Saints for Families

Activity Book

Katherine A. Borgatti

Saints for Families

Saints and me!

Liguori
One Liguori Drive
Liguori MO 63057-9999

Imprimi Potest:
Harry Grile, CSsR, Provincial
Denver Province, The Redemptorists

Published by Liguori Publications
Liguori, Missouri 63057

To order, visit Liguori.org or call 800-325-9521

ISBN 978-0-7648-2296-4

Liguori Publications, a nonprofit corporation, is an apostolate of The Redemptorists. To learn more about The Redemptorists, visit Redemptorists.com.

Printed in the United States of America
18 17 16 15 14 / 5 4 3 2 1
First Edition

How to Use This Book

This book contains reproducible coloring and activity pages to reinforce the stories of the seven saints in the six-volume *Saints and Me!* series, *Saints for Families*: Anthony of Padua, Thérèse of Lisieux, Thomas More, John Bosco, Gerard Majella, and Joachim and Anne. Use each saint's pages as a single lesson, or all together to create hours of entertainment for children. Photocopy these pages for use at home or in the classroom. Answers are provided in the back. After the activity is done, ask the kids to color them in!

Anthony of Padua

hidden pictures

See if you can find:
1 toothbrush
2 stars
3 carrots
4 hearts
5 flowers
6 ladybugs

Veggie Soup

We're making some vegetable soup for dinner, but I'm missing 4 ingredients. Circle 4 things that would make our soup taste delicious.

Connect the dots to finish the picture.

Saint Anthony is a very special saint.
You can write your own little prayer for Saint Anthony,
and maybe even draw him a little picture.

Thérèse of Lisieux

Connect the dots to finish the picture.

Draw the Saint

Draw what you see in each square to make your own portrait of Saint Thérèse.

Help Saint Thérèse find her way to the roses.

Write a prayer to Saint Thérèse here.

Spot the Difference

See if you can spot 6 things that are different about these pictures.

Tic-tac-toesies.

Play a game of tic-tac-toe before the caterpillar eats the posies.

Unscramble the words

These words are all mixed up!

Can you help me unscramble them?

REHETSE___________________

NARCEF___________________

SEORS___________________

TESISRS___________________

VLEO___________________

TAFIH___________________

Thomas more

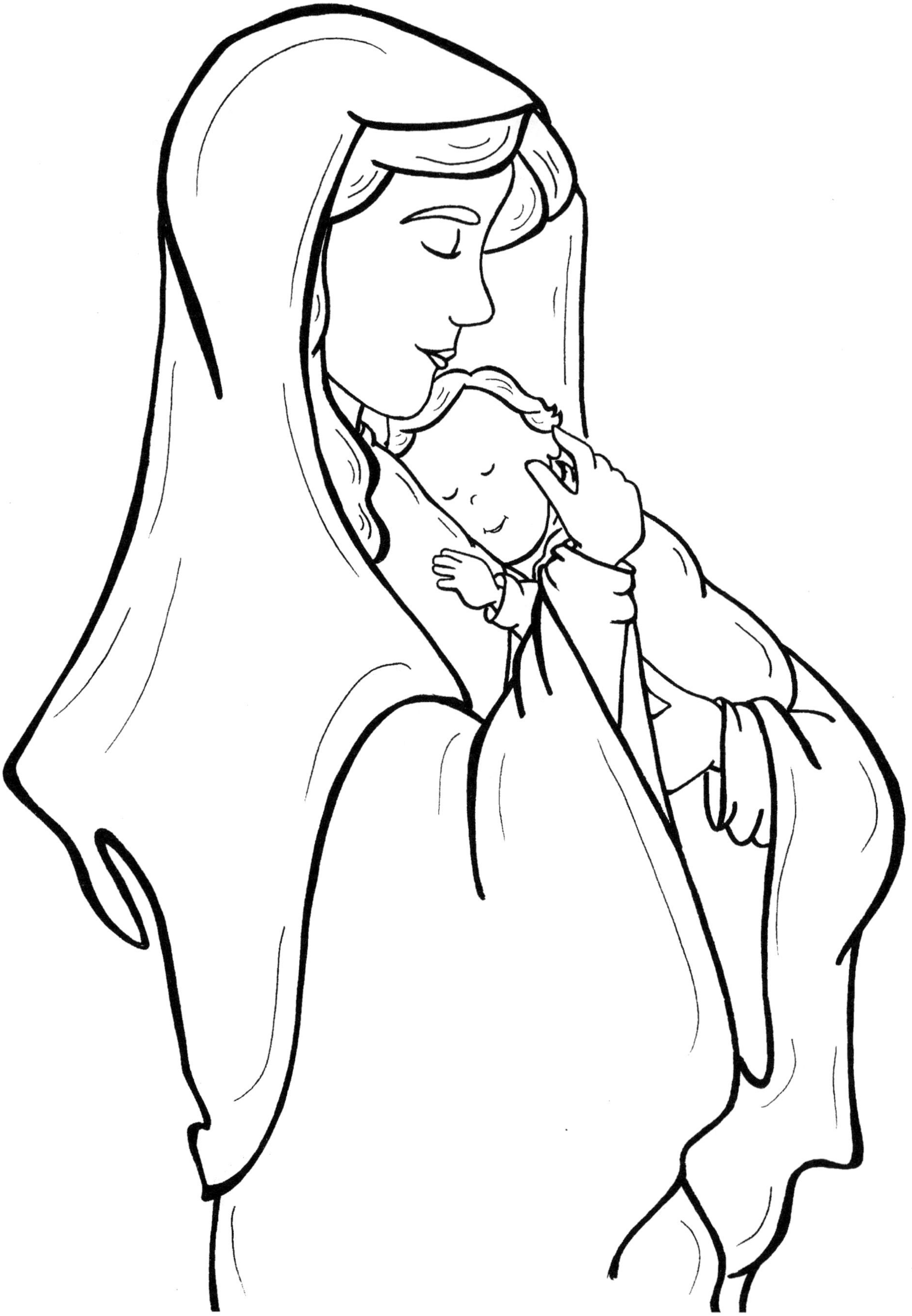

Draw the Saint

Draw what you see in each square to make a picture of Saint Thomas More.

Butterfly Bungalow

This little butterfly needs your help to find his way back home.

Snail-Tac-Toe

Have some fun with a friend and play some tic-tac-toe.

Family Portrait

Saint Thomas More loved his family.

Draw a picture of your family in the frame.

Color it in to make a beautiful family portrait.

Spot the Difference

Circle 6 things that are different on these silly little snails.

Unscramble the Words

These words are all mixed up! Can you help me unscramble them?

OMSAHT____________________

RYLWAE____________________

NGLNDAE____________________

LIFMAY____________________

TOHA____________________

KOMN____________________

John Bosco

Tic-Tac-Birdie

This little bird wants to play some tic-tac-toe.

When you finish the game, you could decorate the grass with flowers or some animal friends for birdie.

These words are all mixed up!

Please help me to unscramble them.

LAITY__________________________ YAPR__________________________

OSBCO__________________________ IDNK__________________________

RTHAFE__________________________ RTOHEM__________________________

Draw the Saint

Draw what you see in each square to make a picture of Saint John Bosco.

Spot the Difference

There are 9 things that are different about these two very special chefs.

Color in the things you see that are different.

The Blessed Virgin Mary was very special to me.

Some words are missing from the beautiful prayer the " Hail Mary".

Can you help me fill in the missing words so we can pray the "Hail Mary" together?

Hail Mary, full of ____________, the __________ is with you;

blessed are you among __________________,

and blessed is the fruit of your womb, ________________.

Holy __________, Mother of ___________,

pray for us sinners

now and at the hour of our death. ____________.

Word Bank:

Amen women Lord Mary Jesus grace God

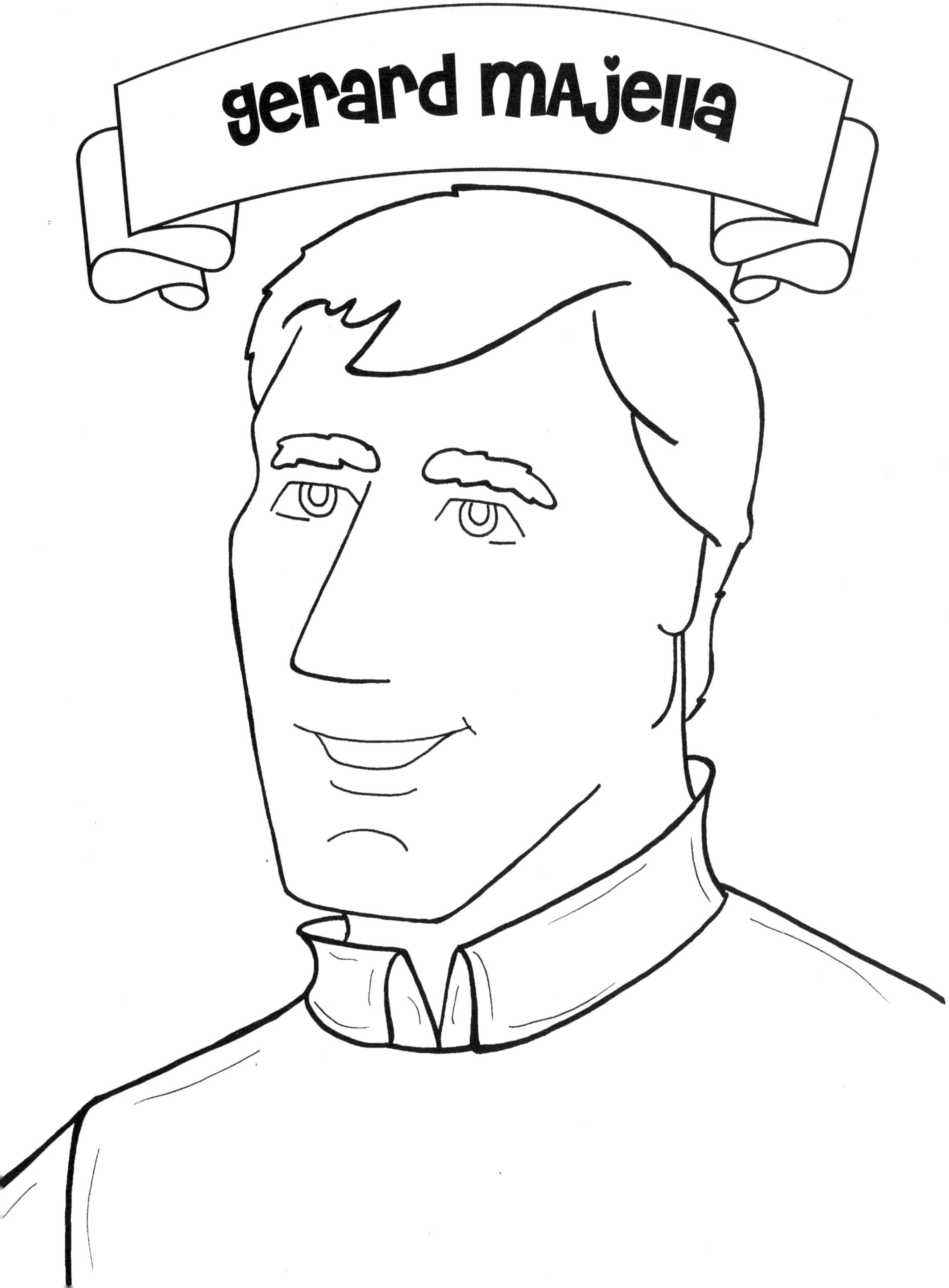
gerard majella

Draw the Saint

Draw what you see in each square to make a picture of Saint Gerard Magella.

I could really use your help.

I was just about to pray the Our Father, but some of the words of this special prayer are missing. Can you fill in the missing words for me?

Our Father, who art in _____________ , hallowed be thy ____________ ;

thy kingdom come; thy will be done on ___________ as it is in ____________.

Give us this day our daily ________ ; and forgive us our trespasses as we forgive

those who trespass against ______ ; and lead us not into ______________ , but

deliver us from ________. Amen.

Word Bank:

name

evil

bread

heaven

temptation

earth

us

Busy Bee's Honey Butter Biscuit Bakery

Busy Bee needs to make his famous honey butter biscuits, but some of the ingredients are mixed up.

Circle the items he needs to bake yummy biscuits.

Busy Bee Tic-Tac-Toe

Find a friend and play a little tic-tac-toe.

Fill the Basket

Saint Gerard brought food to the poor.

What food would you fill this basket with?

Draw and color the food for Saint Gerard's basket.

Saint Gerard was a tailor.

Here are some items that a tailor would use, except......Busy Bee.

See if you can find out where that silly bee is hiding, then color in Saint Gerard and his tailor shop.

BEE'S HIVE

Honey

Joachim and Anne

Draw the Saint

Draw what you see in each square to make a picture of Saint Joachim.

Draw the Saint

Draw what you see in each square to make a picture of Saint Anne.

Connect the Dots

Connect the dots to finish the picture of this fluffy little sheep.

Family Tree

You can make your own family tree.

Draw yourself and your family members in each circle to make a beautiful family tree.

Garden Fun!

Saint Anne loves to work in the garden, but some of these things don't belong in a garden.

Color all of the items you would find or use when working in the garden.

CARROT
PATCH

Answer Key

Veggie Soup: Find 4 missing ingredients.

Connect the dots
to finish the picture.

Connect the dots
to finish the picture.

Help Saint Thérèse find her way to the roses.

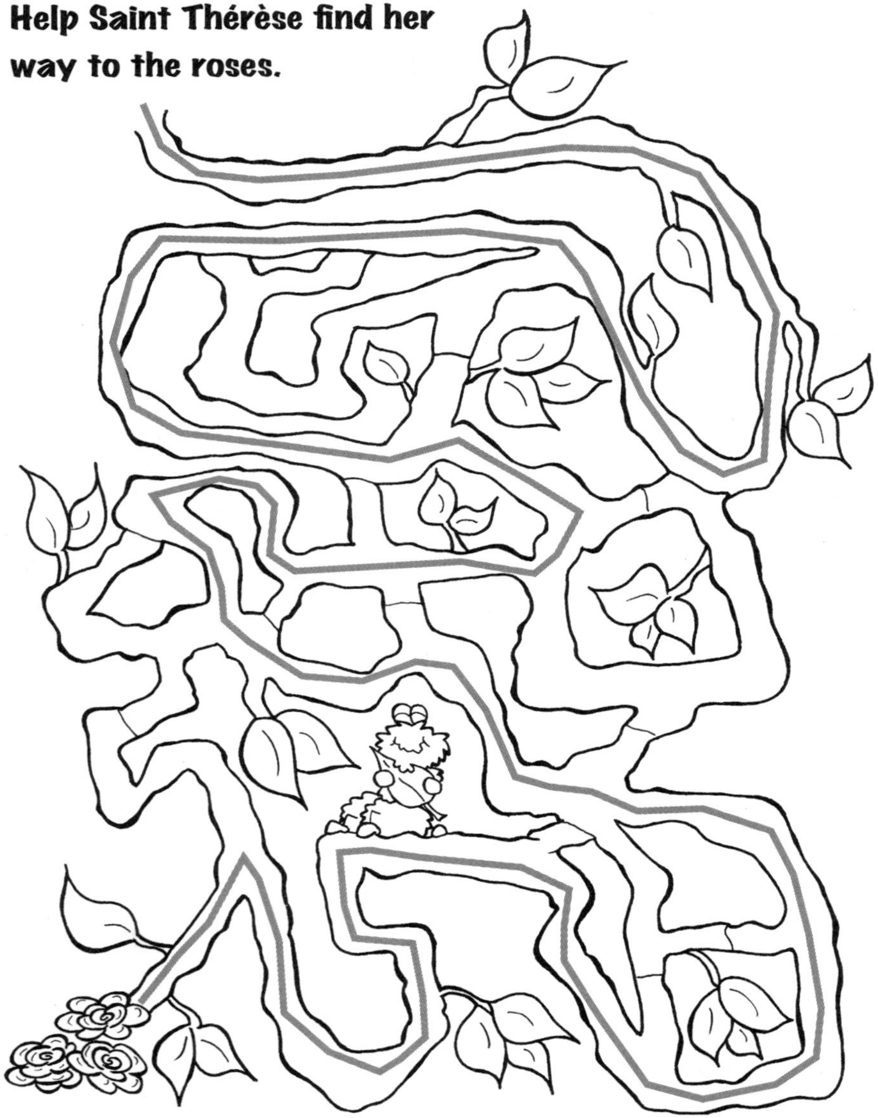

Spot the Difference

See if you can spot 6 things that are different about these pictures.

THERESE

FRANCE

ROSES

SISTERS

LOVE

FAITH

Butterfly Bungalow

This little butterfly needs your help to find his way back home.

Spot the Difference: Circle 6 things that are different on these silly little snails.

Thomas Family

Lawyer Oath

England Monk

The Blessed Virgin Mary was very special to me.

Some words are missing from the beautiful prayer the Hail Mary.

Can you help me fill in the missing words so we can pray the Hail Mary together?

Hail Mary, full of **grace**, the **Lord** is with you;

blessed are you among **women**,

and blessed is the fruit of your womb, **Jesus**.

Holy **Mary**, Mother of **God**,

pray for us sinners

now and at the hour of our death. **Amen**.

I could really use your help.

I was just about to pray the Our Father, but some of the words of this special prayer are missing. Can you fill in the missing words for me?

Our Father, who art in **heaven**, hallowed be thy **name**;

thy kingdom come; thy will be done on **earth** as it is in **heaven**.

Give us this day our daily **bread**; and forgive us our trespasses as we forgive

those who trespass against **us**; and lead us not into **temptation**, but deliver us

from **evil**. Amen.

ITALY	PRAY
BOSCO	KIND
FATHER	MOTHER

Spot the Difference:
There are 9 things that are different about these two very special chefs.

Busy Bee's Honey Butter Biscuit Bakery

Busy Bee needs to make his famous honey butter biscuits, but some of the ingredients are mixed up.

Circle the items he needs to bake yummy biscuits.

Saint Gerard was a tailor. Here are some items that a tailor would use, except......Busy Bee. See if you can find out where that silly bee is hiding. Then color in Saint Gerard and his tailor shop.

Connect the Dots

Garden Fun!

Saint Anne loves to work in the garden, but some of these things don't belong in a garden. Color all of the items you would find or use when working in the garden.

About the Author

Katherine Alpha Borgatti is an artist and illustrator native to Louisiana. She is a convert to the Catholic faith and has a passion for Catholic art. Her works include portraits of Jesus, the Blessed Virgin Mary, and various saints. Katherine has painted a variety of murals, including one for the Louisiana Children's Discovery Center in Hammond, Louisiana. In May of 2010 she completed a children's book that she wrote, illustrated, and published through her company, Painted Daisies Inc.: *Imagination Created*. The slogan "Imagination Created" is designed to encompass the idea that if you can imagine it, we can create it, she says. She also donates her talent to the Catholic church and school that her children attend and visits local schools to do book readings and signings. Katherine lives in Mandeville, Louisiana, with her husband, Mike, and their three children, Matthew, Annamarie, and John.